CATON WOODVILLE'S
TERRITORIAL ARMY
ALBUM

1908

CATON WOODVILLE'S
TERRITORIAL ARMY
ALBUM

1908

YEOMANRY, ARTILLERY, ENGINEERS, AND INFANTRY
WITH THE ARMY SERVICE AND MEDICAL CORPS,
COMPRISING "THE KING'S IMPERIAL ARMY
OF THE SECOND LINE"

The Naval & Military Press Ltd

Published by
The Naval & Military Press Ltd
Unit 10 Ridgewood Industrial Park,
Uckfield, East Sussex,
TN22 5QE England
Tel: +44 (0) 1825 749494
Fax: +44 (0) 1825 765701
www.naval-military-press.com
www.military-genealogy.com
www.militarymaproom.com

Printed and bound in Great Britain by
CPI Antony Rowe, Chippenham and Eastbourne
*In reprinting in facsimile from the original, any imperfections are inevitably reproduced
and the quality may fall short of modern type and cartographic standards.*

ARMY SERVICE CORPS.

LONDON : VIRTUE & CO.

THE GORDON HIGHLANDERS.

LONDON : VIRTUE & CO.

THE BERKSHIRE YEOMANRY

LONDON : VIRTUE & CO

THE ROYAL WELSH FUSILIERS.

LONDON : VIRTUE & CO.

THE ROYAL ENGINEERS (RAILWAY BATTALION.)

LONDON : VIRTUE & CO.

THE DEVONSHIRE REGIMENT. (4th & 5th BATTALIONS.)

LONDON : VIRTUE & CO.

THE BLACK WATCH.
(ROYAL HIGHLANDERS.)

LONDON : VIRTUE & CO.

THE ROYAL SCOTS 4th & 5th BATTALIONS (QUEENS EDINBURGH RIFLES.)

LONDON : VIRTUE & CO.

INFANTRY SKIRMISHING.

LONDON : VIRTUE & CO.

ROYAL GARRISON ARTILLERY

LONDON : VIRTUE & CO.

THE CAMERONIANS (SCOTTISH RIFLES)

LONDON VIRTUE & CO

THE HIGHLAND LIGHT INFANTRY

LONDON : VIRTUE & CO.

ROYAL GLOUCESTERSHIRE HUSSARS

LONDON : VIRTUE & CO

ROYAL ENGINEERS.

LONDON : VIRTUE & CO.

R. Caton Woodville.

THE KING'S (LIVERPOOL REGIMENT.)
10th (SCOTTISH) BATTALION

LONDON : VIRTUE & CO.

THE MANCHESTER REGIMENT.
(6th Battalion has Yellow Facings.)

LONDON VIRTUE & CO.

THE HONOURABLE ARTILLERY COMPANY.

LONDON : VIRTUE & CO.

3rd. COUNTY OF LONDON YEOMANRY.
(SHARPSHOOTERS)

LONDON : VIRTUE & CO.

ROYAL FIELD ARTILLERY.
HOWITZER BATTERY.

LONDON : VIRTUE & CO.

THE LONDON REGIMENT
COUNTY OF LONDON BATTALIONS.

LONDON : VIRTUE & CO.

THE LONDON REGIMENT
COUNTY OF LONDON BATTALIONS.

LONDON : VIRTUE & CO

THE LONDON REGIMENT
CITY OF LONDON BATTALIONS.

LONDON : VIRTUE & CO.

ROYAL ARMY MEDICAL CORPS.

LONDON : VIRTUE & CO

THE NORTHUMBERLAND FUSILIERS.
(4th Battalion has Green Uniform, Scarlet Facings.)

LONDON : VIRTUE & CO

BRIGADIER GENERAL AND STAFF.

LONDON : VIRTUE & CO.

THE PRINCE ALBERT'S (SOMERSETSHIRE LIGHT INFANTRY.)

LONDON : VIRTUE & CO.

ROYAL FIELD ARTILLERY.

LONDON : VIRTUE & CO.

THE QUEEN'S (ROYAL WEST SURREY REGIMENT.)

LONDON : VIRTUE & CO.

THE ROYAL WARWICKSHIRE REGIMENT.

LONDON : VIRTUE & CO.

THE EAST YORKSHIRE REGIMENT.

LONDON : VIRTUE & CO.

PRINCE OF WALES'S OWN WEST YORKSHIRE REGIMENT.
(THE 5th & 6th BATTALIONS.)

LONDON : VIRTUE & CO.

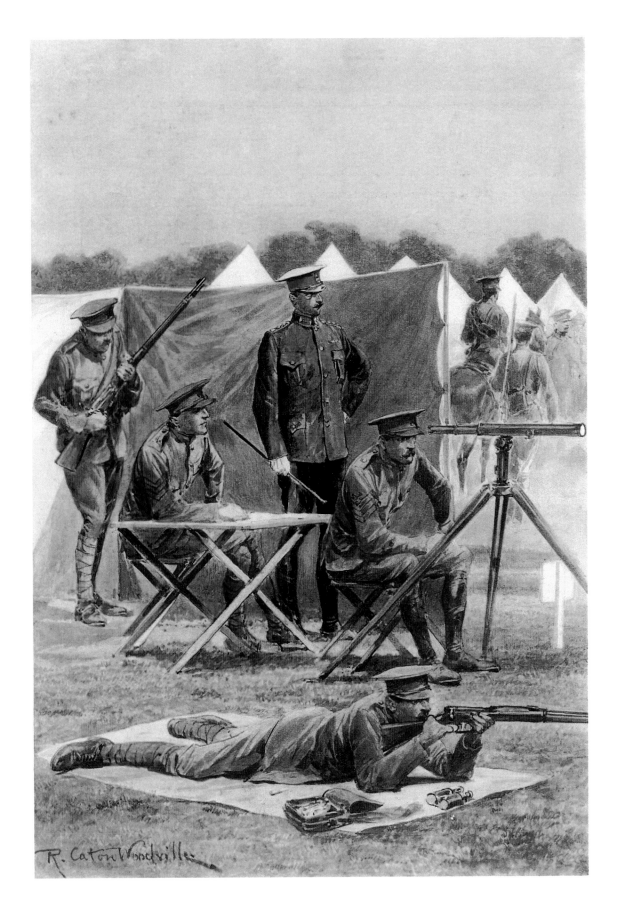

BISLEY.

LONDON : VIRTUE & CO.